You Kiss by th' Book

NEW POEMS

FROM

SHAKESPEARE'S

LINE

GARY SOTO

CHRONICLE BOOKS

SAN FRANCISCO

This book is for my beloved late friend David Ruenzel,
a bard in his own right.

Library of Congress Cataloging-in-Publication Data.

Soto, Gary.
[Poems. Selections]
 You kiss by th' book : new poems from Shakespeare's line / Gary Soto.
  ISBN: 978-1-4521-4829-8
 I. Title.
 PS3569.O72A6 2016
 811'.54—dc23

                     2015025401

Manufactured in China

DESIGNED BY Neil Egan

10 9 8 7 6 5 4 3 2 1

Chronicle Books LLC
680 Second Street
San Francisco, CA 94107
www.chroniclebooks.com

Special quantity discounts are available to corporations and other organizations.
Contact our premiums department at corporatesales@chroniclebooks.com or at
1-800-759-0190.

ACKNOWLEDGMENTS
Several poems have appeared in the *Birmingham Poetry Review* and
Hotel Amerika.

CONTENTS

TWO

THREE

Introduction

What poet doesn't borrow a cup of influence? What poet doesn't sprinkle his or her poetry with the sweet flavor of another's work? I kicked around these thoughts in the used-book store as I read a paperback edition of Shakespeare's sonnets. I hadn't read Shakespeare in years, but here I was— midway through a mundane week, with my reading glasses midway down my nose—when a poem touched me in a way no other poem had touched me in a long time. It was sonnet 18, beautifully tailored, rhythmical in its cadence, true as the moon is true, and instructive in our temporary nature.

> *So long as men can breathe or eyes see*
> *so long lives this, and this give life to thee.*

My heart sighed at this romantic sentiment. At the moment I felt immensely grateful for having rediscovered these sweet lines. What other lines of Shakespeare had I not listened to with the right attention? I kept reading, and the idea formed that it might be fruitful and enjoyable to actively seek out other lines and see how they might inspire me. It was a chance meeting with the bard. I would take a line from Shakespeare and then see where a poem might lead continuing in my own voice.

I wrote this collection in an intense period, during which I read from Shakespeare's plays, sonnets, and poems, my creative antennas swiveling. I thumbed through my college textbook of his complete works. I read two biographies by novelists, not scholars, who admitted to some guesswork when they detailed his everyday wanderings. I worked morning and night, in bed and on the couch, and on occasion with beer in hand on the patio. I went to see two of his plays (California Shakespeare Theater's *The Comedy of Errors* and *The Taming of the Shrew* at the San Francisco Shakespeare Festival, both in 2014) and watched film adaptations of *A Midsummer Night's Dream*, *The Merry Wives of Windsor*, and *Hamlet*. In my car I listened to over-the-top, theatrically delivered sonnets as I tooled around Berkeley and beyond. In short, I was on the hunt for familiar and unfamiliar lines, utterances that might spark a poem. Remarkably, I recognized a change in my language. When had I ever employed words such as "mirth," "prithee," "'tis," and "hast"? I was speaking in a voice from another time!

As I wrote, I envisioned the landscape of sixteenth century English villages with thatched roofs and small garden plots where grew rows of cabbage, carrots, and beans. Chickens and geese patrolled the ground for nibbles, and workers were busy in the hayfields. Or, if not the countryside, I imagined noisy and smoke-laden London Town, where the wagons of peddlers rolled over cobbled street and where, on one tragic day, the wooden houses were destroyed by the Great Fire. There were gallows for the condemned, and stocks where the hapless were ridiculed by passersby. Ships of varying sizes were docked or floating seaward on the Thames. I imagined drunks, yokels, coopers, carpenters, millers, petty thieves, children at play, lovers, city fathers, bewigged lawyers, and jeweled royalty round as barrels. These Elizabethans were kind and then not so kind; they were loving and then not so loving; they were just and then full of revenge as when King Richard shouts, "Shall I be plain? I want the bastards dead."

In writing the poems I played with the punctuation at the end of the line, occasionally using a comma instead of a period or a period instead of a dash, etc. I often found my poems continuing faithful to the emotion and context of the Shakespearean source. If the line hinted at romance, as in "What's in a name? That which we call a rose," I projected romance. If the theme is frustration, as in the hollering line "He hath eaten me out of house and home," I delivered frustration—in this case changing the situation from Mistress Quickly bemoaning Falstaff to a father describing his son's insatiable appetite.

Good readers, here are poems initiated by my love of Shakespeare. They are readable, sincere, possibly quotable, and written under the duress called pleasure. Perhaps the best of each poem is the first line—Shakespeare's— and what follows is all downhill. I don't admonish myself or smirk at my gall.

I make no excuses. This book is for me a worthy undertaking upon which the bard in the hereafter ponders, "Soto . . . Soto . . . 'I smell a device.'"

My device is clear: one line of Shakespeare and then lines from me. With such an approach, I fancy the improbable: that libraries may catalogue us as Shakespeare and Soto, co-authors.

NOTE

The first line of each poem draws from the works of William Shakespeare, often from his plays. I cite the scene, act, and line in this manner: 2.4.16. The reader should be aware that because of the numerous versions of the plays, the quoted lines may not replicate the reader's own copies of the work— my citations correspond to the *Complete Pelican Shakespeare* (2002)—but they'll be close. In the sonnets and poems, I cite the work and the line, as in *Sonnet 11* (14). They will always match.

ONE

The course of true love never did run smooth.

A Midsummer Night's Dream

I'll not budge an inch—
Nay, not an inch if you insist on two.
A coward I am not, or a lily of a man.
Still, I could spare six inches,
Perhaps a foot for good cause,
Three feet, the width of a doorway,
The length of a long fence,
A pathway with afternoon shadows,
The span of a bridge over a tame river . . .

A neighborhood I'll budge,
A borough, the whole of London,
The expanse of a Sussex estate,
Unfenced Stratford, a portion of Wales,
The highlands of Scotland.

I have pride, restraint, and a lion's roar!
I'm determined not to budge an inch,
Unless, little kitty, that inch of my lap belongs to thee.

The Taming of the Shrew (Induction 1.12)

This wish I have, then ten times happy me,

Nine times dancer, eight times wit,

Seven times seamstress, six times nurse,

Five times lady hunter, four times stargazer,

Three times witness to the birthing of lambs,

Two times flirt, one time wedlock with thee.

Sonnet 37 (14)

What's in a name? That which we call a rose
May be a daffodil, a lithe beauty with her own crown,
With her own bee and own dewy light.
Daffodils provide color
And stir the hearts of village girls.

Admittedly, the rose is mightier
For she bends in wind
And arms herself with thorns—
Thus, she is prepared for skirmish.

A girl gives herself in love
When she swings not a milk pail
But her young man's rough and warm hand.

Romeo and Juliet (2.2.43)

Words are no deeds.
A pitcher of cream,
Candles and lace,
A gift of spoons,
The larder bolstered for winter . . .
These are deeds.

But words count for nothing.
I have my own
Smart phrases—
Prithee, Sir Windbag,
Woo me no more.

Henry VIII (3.2.154)

You kiss by th' book,
And I see that you're a poor student.
What chapter did you skip?
Give me your hand
And let's sally to the river
Where the swans glide in pairs
And the deer escape into the myrtle.
I could lay with you, my love.

The prologue may be my lips,
The epilogue my parting knees—
Prince, in this wilderness,
In this crusade of yours,
What kingdom you will find.

Romeo and Juliet (1.5.112)

One half of me is yours, the other half yours,
My thirteen cows reduced by one are still yours,
The chickens reduced by three are yours,
The candles and spoons,
The windows,
The very roof troubled in wind and rain,
The fire I build for you,
All yours.

My footsteps in tilled soil,
The rain that fills these shoeprints,
The plough I captain, the seed I cast,
My labor from morn to dusk . . . all yours.

The Merchant of Venice (3.2.16)

'Tis like a pardon after execution
That you confess, "I did like you."

But, gentlewoman, you also liked cheese
And were not afraid of basted goose.
Soups provided comfort
And peas did roll into your spoon.
And wine? It flowed into your glass
And reddened your cheeks,
Which, I see, have inched down.

True, I loved you for a while,
Three seasons in my youth,
Until I married and fathered children.

But this summery day,
You flirt and say, "I did like you."
But you liked pictures on the wall,
The candlesticks and silver teapots,
The rug by the front door.

Gentlewoman, inspect my healthy brood
Of six children in the yard,
Dirt up to their necks,
Straw behind their ears,
And salty as the sea.
I love them more than my life.

I have my wife, I have my farm.
Two of the chickens go to the block
When the clock strikes three.
Gentlewoman, I could offer you the feathers

From these beheaded chickens—
Like the memory of you,
They weigh almost nothing.

Henry VIII (4.2.121)

My salad days, when I was green in judgment,
And knew not the hearts of men,
Cold as bricks, thick as bricks.

I was a young royal with property,
And green as the grass that feeds on a river,
Green as leaves, green as corn in April.

Fancy men! They smiled
Upon the shine of my silver cutlery,
My teapot, my dinner bell and picture frames.

They visited my stables
And curried my finest horse.
They sized up my lake—trout!
The pheasants scattered from the hedges
When they were shot, puffs of smoke
Like their dreams from muskets.

Smiling, they revealed their teeth,
Yellow as old candles,
Their gums as red as blood.

Yellow and red in the mouths of fancy men?
How they clashed with my green tenderness.

Antony and Cleopatra (1.5.76–7)

The sight of lovers feedeth those in love,
And makes them embrace hotly.
It encourages. It says, "Others feel what we feel,"
And the world is good.

The bee visits the dahlia,
The deer nibbles the hedge,
The trees shake in wind,
And the midday sun makes the wheat sigh.

The strolling lovers come upon other lovers,
The most natural of all mirrors.

As You Like It (3.4.54)

Who alone suffers, suffers most i' the mind,
And here, alas, I speak of a jilted lover.
He suffers not from a severed hand,
A smashed knee, a nose that spilled blood in battle,
Or a beard singed in rescuing a child from fire.

It's love, always love.

The youth absently peels bark from the tree of innocence,
Bark like scabs, the hurt underneath
Raw and bleeding.

King Lear (3.6.103)

What would you have me do?
Untangle the stars and thus our fate?
Pull the grin from the moon's milky face
Or skip after my shadow that sallies ahead?

I love you, and will love you plenty more.
I have a deed to a cottage,
A small tract of land,
A water well and a ditch,
Hills that descend to a brook—
Imagine cows bellowing before dawn!

I love you, and will love you plenty more.
I whisper in your ear
The name of meadow where we may lie
And watch clouds like haystacks—
Their interiors are filled with gentle rain.

Your father, your mother . . . how they mistrust me!
Dear girl, wait for me at the eastern window.
I'll pad quieter than a cat.
If I climb the wall I may rustle the jasmine
And loosen its sweet scent.

My heart swells and spills,
And fills once more—
Dear girl, wait for me at the eastern window,
For I'll be like the sun just climbing up,
Bright with love for thee.

Pericles (4.6.163)

For ever and a day
My love declared his love.
He spoke truth in "day,"
For he was gone by Sunday.
His parting gift arrived nine months later.
The babe cries, feeds, and cries yet again.

Poor, ignorant me . . .
Is it this what he meant by "forever"?

As You Like It (4.1.135)

All that glisters is not gold.
A ruby ring winks, the silver cutlery shines,
The blood-red sapphire hangs in splendor,
And you, good lady, walk in nature.

Carrying a rose, you blossom.
Biting into a peach, you scent the air.
Dipping a foot in the pond,
You shackle your ankle with diamond-like beads.

Rose, peach, diamond-like beads . . .
This is your wealth and youth your beauty.
With a garland in your hair
The golden hue of bees follows.

The Merchant of Venice (2.7.65)

A stage, where every man must play a part,
Is rough place for the swashbuckler.

He rates not as an actor.
He rates not as a lover.
But he does rate as a lonely mouse
Nibbling his whiskers!

On my splintery stage of life,
Before an audience of pigeons
Splattered with mud,
The swashbuckler shed real tears
When the maiden he loved sang "No."

The Merchant of Venice (1.1.78)

Love will not be spurred to what it loathes.
Young husband brighten your complexion

And consider the country lovers in a tangle
And repeat the sweet favors at home.

The Two Gentlemen of Verona (5.2.7)

Shall I compare thee to a summer's day?
You are bright-skinned and graceful,
And you are the fields in your sway.
Almond-eyed, pouty and naked by a river . . .
I close my eyes and see you!
You are the second sister among four,
And more beautiful than all three on their best days.
Your left cheek is a peach,
And the right cheek yet another peach.

Darling, I beseech you to give me your hand.
Or if not your hand then your pinkie,
Delicate little hook that shall reel me in.

Sonnet 18 (1)

This above all: to thine own self be true.
Alas, I confess that I am not true to myself but to you—
The stars reveal this, the mighty oak and the rose,
The flinty rocks I skipped across a brook.

I have walked my loneliness to the sea,
And the sea roared in both ears.
I swallowed and tasted sadness.
I lay in the grass and closed my eyes—
I saw only you, in a dress white as a cloud.

Admittedly, I'm not as tall as thee,
Neither smart as thee, nor rich as thee.
Yet, my dear lamb,
Let me be your admirer.
I am a stable boy,
You a rich farmer's daughter.
Let me be like wheat in wind, bending just so,
Not the weak-stemmed daffodil, bent in rain,
Dipping its face in mud churned by a workman's clogs.

Hamlet (1.3.77)

Most true it is that I have looked on truth
And found no wealth in it,
No prospect of acquiring fields
Or the very beasts of these fields.
Truth keeps you poor as a mouse
And colors you the same—
Gray, with only whiskers to nibble.

Truth is God, a distant friend they say.
But for me I prefer a country girl
Who'll fiddle with my belt, lay down willingly,
And point her lusty legs to the sky,
Most true, most true.

Sonnet 110 (5)

The more I give to thee, the more I have.

As you are my wife, I give thee the thatch on the roof,

You give to me the pot's piping soup.

The sheep I give thee,

The cow's milk and the rooster's crow.

The rows of beans you offer,

The lettuce and the turnip,

The carrot long as a dog's tail,

The hot potato on a fork,

All the harvesting of love.

To thee, I give apples and my love all summer.

In spring, you give me the rose of a child.

Romeo and Juliet (2.2.134−5)

Men's flesh preserved so whole do seldom win.

Where's the cut and slash, the ridge of scar,

The pucker fashioned by iron,

The toe split by a wheel,

The twig of bent finger,

The chin cracked by an iron glove?

Where's the retired knee,

Or the eye that weeps for France?

Men who fight bravely often win,

Though in love may suffer defeat:

Inside the shirt of one tested corporal,

The heart pumps a pale and weakened blood.

His injury is the worst of all—

A beauty slew him on the spot

When she uttered, "Kind sir, be gone."

2 Henry VI (3.1.301)

Need and oppression starveth in thy eyes,
And on your cheeks
Hollowed hunger.

Hot soup for you, bread that will stick,
And love, love, spoonfuls of love.

Romeo and Juliet (5.1.70)

My thoughts are whirlèd like a potter's wheel:
I love her, I love her more, and I love her more than . . .
O dear, the wheel doth flick
Mud in my eye.

1 Henry VI (1.7.19)

Get thee a good husband, and use him as he uses thee.
To his soup add meat, carrots, and the tears of an onion.
Remember to keep the teapot on the stove,
The biscuit a sweet thing to crumble,
And butter to make him melt.

By candlelight or by moonlight,
He loves you in all places.
Night is best, with a window partly opened
For the gossipy neighborhood
To hear love's thrashing.

When he's out of his boots,
Your husband is not tall.
His hat is but a basket of all his dreams
And his loveliest dream is of you.
Marriage is such sweet porridge.
In bed, you come first and ask for seconds.

All's Well That Ends Well (1.1.212–13)

Pitchers have ears,
Spoons valleys,
The kettle a whistle,
Tongs a bite,
And the shiny plate
A natural portion
For meat and potatoes.

The shoe has a kick,
The belt a snap,
The vest a hug,
And the button,
Detached, currency
When a good woman
Threads the needle.

The Taming of the Shrew (4.4.52)

Take him and cut him out in little stars,
And toss him skyward! He's my dear love,
My darling, the envy of night.

Let him shine!
He's my tiara, my twinkle.

Let me roll in bed. Let me sleep!
If mine eyes stir behind their lids,
They do move in search of him.

Romeo and Juliet (3.2.22)

That comfort comes too late,
And love not at all. Embers blink
In the hearth and soon
This fire grows cold.
I'm with my misery,
My needlework,
A thread of nothing.

I bore four children
And two sleep forever
As babes in their graves.
When wind howls
It's their crying
To get up—
They've slept enough.
Poor twins they were,
Water in their lungs
As they drowned
At the shores
Of pneumonia.

My husband sits in his chair
And he reads the Bible
Until he falls asleep.
Unsightly, so unsightly . . .
With head back,
His mouth is open
And his snore does trumpet.
It's the only music
I'm given all day.

Henry VIII (4.2.120)

We would, and we would not
Marry in April amid the blossoms sailing downstream.
We would marry in May when the bee revisits the rose,
Or June when the strawberries first appear.
In July we would marry,
In August when peaches swell,
When grapes are bursting.
In September, October, November . . .

Darling, let's marry in February,
When we leave the church, my hand in yours,
A celebration of snowflakes will fly about us—
How warm the bed,
How pink your breasts,
How our love
Begets an early spring.

Measure for Measure (4.4.32)

Love is blind, and lovers cannot see
When they frolic on the grass—
A button is undone, the ribbon cast aside.

When they look up, pink cheeked,
They see trees, boulders, each other's youth—
And a farmer thin as a sapling tree,
With a pitchfork and stung from envy.

The Merchant of Venice (2.6.36)

TWO

Thereby hangs a tale.

As You Like It

What is the opinion of Pythagoras concerning wildfowl?

That they wing south in winter, north in summer,

That they tweet for pleasure,

That they narrow their eyes when stroked,

That they clack their beaks before they feast,

That they drink from their own lean tracks,

That they are sleek and colored splendidly,

That they float like cork.

They are delightful à l'orange,

And their wings will pull free like stockings.

The plucked and noble wildfowl offers feathers

For your pillow and this, my good fellow,

Explains your dream of flying.

Twelfth Night (4.2.49–50)

You blocks, you stones,
You children of mine
Now turned thieves!
You stole bread
And apples
Until you were caught—
What, the belt in youth
Did not sting enough?

You blocks, you stones,
The jailor will grind you to dust
And carry you away in wind.
As for my punishment,
May this dust fly into my eyes
And blind me.

Julius Caesar (1.1.35)

Being fond on praise, which makes your praises worse,

How are we to believe you?

You praise the apple and the pie equally,

And walnuts you like, the strawberries and blueberries.

You praise Sunday but Monday is also a favorite,

And spring is delicious and summer heady with sumptuous clouds.

You cuddle a kitten and cuddle a baby—what's the difference?

Praise to the scholar and his opposite, the imbecile!

Praise to the manor on the hill and the manor in the valley!

Praise to the Protestants and the Catholics with their trinkets!

Praise to the goat for, as do you, the beast likes everything.

Sonnet 84 (14)

The evil that men do lives after them
And is found in politics. The statesman says,
"My palms itch." Thus, we must pay.

But good men do dwell in tombs.
These saints did not itch, they did not lie,
They did not budge a clackety bone
For dishonest work.

Passed on, evil seethes and grows.

Julius Caesar (3.2.76)

Drunk? and speak parrot?
Speak hog and cow,
And the fourth language, donkey?
Drink makes us sing and brag,
And if the corks fly,
If the brew foams
In tankers,
Then we revel
And recount our journeys,
All fanciful tales.
We recount lasses
Who loved us
In spite of our stink
And drab cloaks.
We recount bears
Who chased us into trees
So tall we could
See the Isle of Wight
From such heights—
Improbable babble
That makes us slap our knees.

Drunk, we speak parrot,
Hog and cow,
Dog and rooster,
And toward morning
Bray the language of donkeys.

Othello (2.3.268)

The fault and glimpse of newness,
The first impression,
As when the earl arrived tall as a door,
Feather in hat, sword with a single jewel,
And in boots up to his knees—
He had seen war, journeyed to Arabia,
Wooed Italian beauties by plucking a guitar.
You mused: now here is valor,
Here is truth, here is handsomeness!

When this noble man rubbed his hands
At the hearth and meowed, "I'm cold,"
He showed himself a kitten dressed as a rake,
One who preferred not ale or wine
But milk to stain his whiskers white.

Measure for Measure (1.2.157)

The naked truth of it is, I have no shirt.
Presently, my shoes squeak from holes,
And my britches are held up by a clothespin—
My belt, I bartered for a pie.

And let us not speak of the hat that flew like straw,
The frock lost in a roll of dice,
Or my father's ring hocked for lodging.

My teeth went, then my hair.
My eyes leak from their own piping sorrow.
Though plentiful air is all around,
I'm winded when I step three paces.

O poverty, I came into this life naked
And naked I'll go out.

Love's Labor's Lost (5.2.700)

The time will come that foul sin, gathering head,
Shall meet a greater sin. Together,
They will gather other sins
To compile a book of them,
All foul testimonies,
Epilogue after epilogue.

From sins shall be bred great poets.

2 Henry IV (3.1.76)

They come not single spies, but in battalions,
These flies that grope my dinner meat,
And bring on their thinner cousins, the gnats.
The gnats whine at my ears and before my eyes,
But admittedly they give better counsel
Than the fools I employ.

Summer! The fruits invite these winged pests.
I tire of them. Where is autumn
That will draw them away,
And winter that will freeze them!
And presently . . . the needle-nosed mosquito,
Which dips freely into my flesh.

Do these pests not know I'm king?
I possess no sword small enough to kill them,
Though I do strike them with my palm.
Yet, they return, like conspirators.

Flies, gnats, and mosquitoes,
A beard of their kind on my face,
A shadow of their kind behind me,
A crown of their kind on my head!

If there were more battalions,
They would lift my kingdom from me!

Hamlet (4.5.78–9)

Who so firm that cannot be seduced?
The consumptive steals a pie,
The parson a halfpenny,
The washerwoman a row of buttons,
The widow a candle and all its drippings.

Who drinks from the wine chalice?
Who creeps away with a basket of apples?
Who lifts eggs from a warm nest?

We steal in small increments.
In the kitchen, the dog licks a dirty pot,
And the fly scrubs its face into an apple paring.
The nail is pulled from a board.
A shingle hidden behind a blouse.
And the boat at the wharf?
You'll find it downstream.

And what's up the kitchen helper's sleeve?
A biscuit for his love,
Lass who waddles among the geese.
Her hair is straw-colored
And on a bed of straw she'll slumber.

Who is sinless, who is not a thief?
For a lark, the clouds steal away the sun
And for days will not bring it back.

Julius Caesar (1.2.312)

This fellow is wise enough to play the fool.
I ask, "Prithee, how is thy father?"
The fool shrugs and pushes a finger into his nose—
Lord, the glob is a meal for three!

"Thy mother's gout," I inquire, "much improved?"
He gazes heavenward—geese and a chevron
Of other flappers. With my head raised,
I cringe at the reeking drift from the tannery
And gaze at a ship docking in the harbor.
I level my attention on this boy,
Possibly brought into this troubled world feet first.

"Your sister," I lastly inquire,
And he squeals and pats his belly.
With child? I wonder. Then a fruit cart
Bumps down this narrow path,
And the boy pushes me aside
To give it room. In his nudging,
He lifts my purse from my cloak,
Or so I discover later in my rooms.
O, at first I was frantic at the loss
And then laughed hardily.
I looked out the window—
More geese, more chevrons,
Another cart, thieving boys on every corner.

Old man, brow with lines remembered from books,
His schooling today was learned from the street.

Twelfth Night (3.1.59)

'Tis time to fear when tyrants seem to kiss,
The lamb sides with the wolf,
The cat saddles a hound,
The lark carols to the snake,
The pig trots briskly to its death,
And you, rabble-rouser,
Have the last say—your head three days
On a spike adorns the city wall . . .

With your mouth hanging open,
Flies do all the speaking.

Pericles (1.2.79)

To have seen much and to have nothing
Is to say that you gobbled the sights of the world
And now are blind! Look at you—
Wasted by poverty!
The babe has more food on his bib
Than your pantry hoards for winter!
You eat from the chipped plate of experience
While we who worked banquet merrily.

You watched the rivers flow past
And took not a fish,
Though the fish showed you their fins:
The rich widow begged, "Be mine,"
The journeyman said, "Work for me, son."
Fool! You boarded a ship
And saw the world three times
When once was enough.

O wayward knave, look upon the farms.
Scarecrows have more stuffing than thee.

As You Like It (4.1.22)

Nothing will come of nothing
And this I have squirreled away
In my pocket—nothing.
Yet, like a coin,
It supplies my daily bread.

I have nothing,
But do barter it on my knees
At Black Friar's bridge.

You would be surprised
How nothing fills me up.

King Lear (1.1.90)

He can speak French; and therefore he is a traitor.
He can speak the King's English; and therefore he's a lawyer.

Run from both! The traitor points you out
And the lawyer serves a bill for your defense.

2 Henry VI (4.2.168–9)

To say there is no vice but beggary
Allows me an income when I ask,
"A crust of bread, my dear sir."
I'm a failed tailor, a failed father—
In fear of me, my children outran the mice.
My wife returned to her mother,
And together they died
Holding hands—consumption.

A beggar who plays the whistle earns little,
As he must compete with birds
Who work for crumbs, not loaves.

The vice for begging bread?
The shadow of my begging hand
Is cleaner than the hand itself.

King John (2.1.596)

What village, friends, is this?
The donkey wears a crown,
The mayor a harness.
The jailor the monk's habit,
And, with a Hey Nonny Nonny,
The thief pares an apple
Under a glorious tree.

Twelfth Night (1.2.1)

By the pricking of my thumbs,

By the weather report in my bones,

By my hair that departed before I was thirty,

By my five children and my two dead wives,

By my life I declare, honorable judge, my innocence.

Neither the pig nor cow did I steal.

They arrived in my yard because of lightning.

Truly, these beasts feared for their dumb lives.

By the rivers in my palm,

By my tongue that recalls a prayer,

By the scent of burning leaves (the lightning!),

By my belly that is always present (I'm fat as a barrel),

By the angels that visit, by the devil that frets,

By, again, my five children and two dead wives,

By my life I declare my innocence

For I have no taste for rustled pig or cow.

Macbeth (4.1.66)

Can honor set to a leg? No. Or an arm? No.
Can honor straighten the humpback grocer?
Iron out a ploughman's finger hurt by age?

Can honor dispatch the purplish gout?
Can honor make the blind see?
Can honor retie the knot of a maidenhead?

Distrust the fellow who speaks of honor.
For surely he's a politician
Who speaks from both sides of his mouth
And, once elected, from the pucker of his arse.

1 Henry IV (5.1.131–2)

Every man has his fault, and honesty is his,
As when the youthful cadet reported to the captain,
"Sir, the coins are gone." He spoke of a purse
Taken off a sailor hooked from the river Thames.

The captain looked upon the honest youth,
And absorbed every bit of his nature—
Let me not trust this boy, let me not forget him.
The captain walked away. Coins jingled in his pocket
When he departed the morgue, stairs worn
From dead men's heels slapping against stone.

Timon of Athens (3.1.26)

He jests at scars that never felt a wound.
He laughs at the actor though lacks the gift of words.
He trips a beggar but borrows his cloak.
He cries for war but creeps away before dawn.

He kicks a sleeping dog.
When the owner appears
He whistles and studies the clouds.

He sweats that never lifted a hoe.
He speaks ill of the king but pounces on his coin.
He marries first but quickly drops his britches for a widow.

This lackey is false,
As wood is true, as iron is true,
As rain that doth wonders in the fields.
He says one thing,
But by actions says another
If a better wind doth blow.

Romeo and Juliet (2.2.1)

But for mine own part, it was Greek to me.
His hands spoke clearer than his words.
They flew about like gesturing birds
Until I understood that he had sardines
For sale. The fisherman pointed
To the basket and turned back the cloth:
Like acrobats, the frisky sardines leapt,
All alive, fresh from sea,
With mouths gasping.

I pouched five sardines,
Each with a single eye on me,
And brought them home.
The cat spoke up.
This sneaky fellow I understood—
Dancing on his hind legs,
The little rascal got a head,
Two slippery fins,
And from my boot
A gentle nudge out the door.

Julius Caesar (1.2.283–84)

He hath not drunk ink,
This knave who knows not books.
He knows not nature and the nature of horses.
Yet, he climbs onto a horse
And faces not ahead but backward,
Rump fitting poorly in the saddle.
True, if he spurred this horse,
He would gallop homeward.
By the trail of horse droppings
The knave would learn more than we
About beasts and filthy roads.

Love's Labor's Lost (4.2.25)

An honest tale speeds best being plainly told,
And, good fellow, I ask how is it
You are dressed in rags?
Did your father box your ears?
Did your mother sing a tune
Of belt whippings across thy legs?
The school master, the Dutch nuns in wooden clogs . . .
That they lash you with rope?
Perhaps an older brother stole your daily grub,
Or a thief robbed you?
Ill advice from a drunken priest perhaps?
Or is your pitiful state is result
Of the war with France,
Or your years in commerce—
Indeed, that must be it! Your partner fled
With the wealth of your noble work!

Nay, by the hollowness of your cheeks,
I fear thy wife left you for a soldier . . .
A tradesman who deals trinkets?
Nay, a lawyer—the worst people
Except when you need them.

Ay, sir, be honest! It's the result of plague?
My arrow of thought has hit the target!
You recovered in body but lost all—
Wife and children, house and business.
If I'm wrong, tell me, but make it brief.
How is it that you possess but one shoe?
That your coat is the flag of defeat?
That your shirt is an oily rag?
That the dirt around your neck

Could grow carrots and potatoes?
How is that your right eye
Is half closed, and a tear the size
Of a pebble adorns your cheek?
Though I chatter like a bird,
O please confess to your friend,
If 'twas the fire that ravaged London!
The poor fellow swallowed,
Examined his palms for his fate,
And answered the rich man
In his three-button coat.

"Bird chatter," I agree, "you talk and talk.
My tale is simple, feathered one:
I am but lazy."

Richard III (4.4.358)

How shalt thou hope for mercy, rendering none?
How shalt thou expect love, if thou not love in return?

How shalt thou live, if what you do is but yawn?
How shalt thou express kindness, if a dog striker you be?

How shalt thou fan a fire, if no match is lit?
How shalt thou farm, if dirt is not your kin?

Let me tell you! You are a miser in all ways!
My lesson is this: a sober farmer with mercy and love,

With a dog that will paddle into the lake,
With a fire in the hearth, is the noblest of men.

The Merchant of Venice (4.1.88)

If money go before, all ways do lie open,
As when the carriage stops
And out steps a lord with his wig off center,
His eyes stingily half-closed,
For why should he share his self-love
And open them fully?
He sniffs at the street's foulness—
What horse pile in the road is this?
What beggar? What shoeless child?

The lord is moneyed,
A relic in the church,
A canker to the Hammersmith whore.
Yet, when the tailor's door opens
And with a click closes behind him,
He acquires fine gabardine or heavy wool,
For when he sweats,
When he emits his human smell,
He has no intention of parting with either—
Why should he let others share
What he alone hath paid for?

The Merry Wives of Windsor (2.2.160)

I have a touch of your condition,
The bitter liver, the breath of deceit,
Bone spurs and pink eye,
The knob of anger,
A hammer toe that kicks,
A worm of bile that inches along.
I suffer from a sparking tooth
And a tongue that bites like a rat.
My turnip nose, my chin that is a spade,
My wobbly ladder of legs.
And madness? I wore a friar's robe
For three years, and that wooly cloth
Made me itch from head to foot.

To hide my illness,
I wear black garments.
When a child stares at me,
I stare back with an awful grin,
A foul hole of a mouth,
And spout a sewer of words
That soils his trousers
And scares him home.

Richard III (4.4.158)

My pride fell with my fortunes.
It rose again when I discovered

Poor was not such a bad coin.

As You Like It (1.2.239)

Neither a borrower nor a lender be,
Except for mine enemy. I could lend him the tip
Of my dagger and quickly take it back—
The blood he sheds was only borrowed at birth.

Hamlet (1.3 74)

He hath eaten me out of house and home,
This tall son of mine.
He has devoured the Sunday chicken on Friday,
The puddings and tarts, the meat pies,
The bread and apples,
The grapes that are mostly water
But priced like gold . . .

What will his appetite start on next?
The candles and their stiff drippings?
The walls he shall lick? The leaded glass,
The straw beds, the wooly scarves on a hook?
If I feel a tug on my sleeve,
Is it his nibbling teeth?
And I dare not remove my slippers—
He will unravel my socks
To the last thread!

Woe is me! When he was a lad
And in the countryside,
I shouldn't have introduced the goat,
A poor model of deportment.

My son eats his fill
And eats some more,
The goat's favorite meal
My very last straw!

2 Henry IV (2.1.72)

I am a great eater . . .

And I believe that does harm to my wit.

And wine does not help,

Or mine eating the bagpipe of a sheep's stomach.

Last night I ate, drank and danced before the hearth,

And pressed a coin into a servant's palm

When the clock struck three.

I fell into bed, and the world did spin.

I chucked up drink and pudding.

I did an encore an hour later,

The spillage hitting not the flowery bowl but the floor.

I rose at noon to the cutting nature of the sun.

I was very stupid, I was very thirsty.

As such, I faintly remembered my name, title,

And estate that rolls from east to west.

Outside my window,

Sheep like almighty bagpipes.

I moaned for a pitcher of river water,

And for those burly trotters to please quiet.

I sat on the edge of my bed, head lowered,

And in time stared at the creature in the mirror—

O dear me, mutton for cheeks.

Twelfth Night (1.3.81–2)

But yet I run before my horse to market.
My haste takes away my hair,
The wind in my lungs. I hurry,
And to what purpose? It's still dark,
With the morning dew yet to seep
From the earth and moisten the grass.

My horse trots behind,
The cart small as a coffin,
The apples bouncing on unclean hay.
I smell commerce, while my horse,
His nostrils flared, smells the greed in me.

Richard III (1.1.160)

The king was weeping-ripe for a good word.
A flatterer, I approached in soft slippers
And remarked heartily, "The crown sparkles."
He looked up, his eyes like rain at a hard hour,
And pointed me to stand by the fire —
Nay, in the fire, as he called me a devil!

The hearth was like a bear's roaring mouth,
And its tongue of flame did tickle my ears.

Love's Labor's Lost (5.2.275)

It lies as coldly in him as fire in a flint
When the village sot wittingly strikes
A spark of conversation,
And blows his hardy laughter
Between candle-like teeth.
Tonight, he speaks of the Queen
And Queen's lap dog,
Powdered head, powdered tail, powdered paws . . .

Laughter from the parson,
Laughter from the doctor and the barber.

A story is merrier when the ale flows free.

Troilus and Cressida (3.3.256)

Rich gifts wax poor when givers prove unkind,
As when the prosperous farmer tosses a bone.

In mud, it splashes; in a puddle, it splashes.
The delivery is rough. The bone is meatless,

Horseshoe-shaped, sucked of the marrow.
We dogs sniff at the farmer's gift, circle it twice,

And knowing what is kind and unkind
Raise a short leg for a hot squirt.

Hamlet (3.1.101)

We must not make a scarecrow of the law.
Citizens, let the law rise naturally strong,
And be fed mutton, fowl, and stern mead.
Gloved or ungloved, law's hand should be mighty,
His jaw square, his eye fiery, his arm veined,
Not like the scarecrow who gives up
His innards when a paltry wind doth blow.

Measure for Measure (2.1.1)

For they say an old man is twice the child,
That he harps for milk, then ale.

Having no teeth, the old man slurps porridge
And farts when he sneezes.

He reads not, he thinks even less.
His buttons are in the wrong holes.

If he had more hair on his ears,
The chirping birds would nest there.

Twice the child, twice the trouble,
Two times he will taste a thing

To judge it good or bad.

Hamlet (2.2.328)

There's many a man hath more hair than wit,
And more sight than vision.
His coin-jiggling steps are long but his circuit short.
He's a brute first, and a brute second.
He pulls his wife's hair, paddles his children,
And mutters at the parson to hurry the sermon.

He smells the rose, but what of it?
Its sweetness is not his,
For he is an uncouth brute!
He knows not that the rose is beauty
Or that his wife is sweet as sugar.

Brutes! Why do they live, and live so well?
The petals fall, the wind snaps,
A dot of rain taps the onlooker's head for an answer.

The Comedy of Errors (2.2.81–2)

To kings that fear their subjects' treachery
Let them not sleep, eat, or love their queens.
Let the kings pace their chambers
And their unconcerned subjects frolic in the parks.

The kings warred for kingdoms,
And presently worry about gout.
Let the subjects roust themselves
From bed at their slow pleasure.
Let the day begin not at dawn but midday—
Behead the rooster that crowed,
And toss his spurs over a fence.

The best kingdom? When the king is drunk,
The priest drunker, and the taxman the drunkest of all.
Only then do the subjects get on as they please.

3 Henry VI (2.5.45)

To one not sociable
Take yourself outdoors
Where the deer nibbles myrtle,
The gopher pinches the carrot,
And the bear rounds out his belly—
Alas, poor bear, his fur will soon
Be spread before the hearth.
The wind will roar
Down the flue
And spark the embers
Of civilized talk.

Cymbeline (4.2.13)

The colt that's backed and burdened being young
Goes not far, for he has no spirit.
He has but a routine of grinding corn.

He eats little, drinks even less.
Flies scrub his eyelids when he doth cry.

Venus and Adonis (419)

Have is have, however men do catch.
Thus I borrow on one corner,
Steal on two, beg on three,
And on the fourth corner
Sell what I've got.

King John (1.1.173)

THREE

GLOUCESTER: O, let me kiss that hand!

LEAR: Let me wipe it first, it smells of mortality.

King Lear

Who chooseth me, must give and hazard all he hath,
Be it his fields and the beasts of his fields,
Be it the oak and the birds that dwell in the oaks,
His riches in the jingle of coins,
His health that doth work his lungs,
His steps that mark a straight path,
His love for wife and children,
His hound that noses a friendly hand.

Who chooseth me seeks momentary fortune.
He desires earthly things now, and now, and now.
They're his as long as the candle flickers,
By which I mean that candle in his house
And the one in his heart.
At death, he hazards becoming mine.

The Merchant of Venice (2.7.9)

Th' inaudible and noiseless foot of time,
Small footed it is, a pacer in quilted slippers.
We age, grow saggy mouthed—
The key is in your hand
And you ask, "Now what purpose is this?"

The house creaks,
The fire is stirred like mush,
And in the smoky kitchen
The mice pinch herbs for bedding.
The candle flickers, the kitten leaps in her play—
The daily merriments will continue after we're gone.

We should pace wisely,
For to rush means to arrive at the end—
Who wishes a root to grow through his eye?

Time is sand poured through a shapely glass.
Time is the small hammer inside a clock.
Time is the sunlight bleeding through a church window.
Time is in the weathervane,
The squeak of its screw.

And you, a widower,
Shuffler and borrower,
Noisy neighbor with far too many chickens,
Prepare yourself. Time is slow, quick, then not at all.

All's Well That Ends Well (5.3.41)

What do you read, my lord?

Words that break like oaths,
Sentences as long as snakes,
Verses that end in a sigh,
And you, true scholar
With lines on your brow,
A parable of pitiful sorrow.

Hamlet (2.2.191)

Youth's a stuff will not endure.
And better that it ends,
For who wishes to be villainously old?
Youth is love, beauty,
And 'tis the quick step
Over a mirroring puddle.

Youth's spring, and a summer,
When the bees touch the primrose
And profit from its sweetness.
Rain brings forth the wheat that we may live.

O how life is seven inches a candle!
O how the river never tires!
O how the geese roll through thunder!

Fathers! Mothers! You spinsters too!
Youth went with the summering geese.
Clouds the color of gravestones
Are paddling our way!

Twelfth Night (2.3.50)

There comes the ruin, there begins confusion,
There comes the mayor in his fur-collared robe
And mayor's page tooting a whistle.

There comes the soldier, there comes the physician,
There comes the prince
And the prince's hangers-on.

The world parades on a pebbled road
One end to the next—the sun is up,
Life is short, grab what you will.

There comes the yokel and the yokel's tallest son,
There comes the watchmaker in a dark coat
And his sluggish wife behind.

There comes the potter, there comes the parson,
There comes the hurdy-gurdy man
And his monkey on a chain.

The world parades on a pebbled road
One end to the next—the sun is up,
Life is short, grab what you will.

1 Henry VI (4.1.194)

This disease is beyond my practice,
Gentlewoman. I'm familiar with bones splintered by a fall
And on the properties of blood I have an opinion.
The rash between toes, the tongue split by too much talk,
Gout and consumption, the finger like a bent nail,
The leg short of perfect . . .
Of these I'm knowledgeable,
And, I may add, the art of wrapping the dead in linen.
For the throat, I shake a secret powder into your brew.
For cramps, I keep tea in a locked box.
For the pangs of childbirth, I have my two hands.

But guilt is not my business.
When you speak of one king killed
And another crowned,
Could we call this destiny? You're a peacock
That drags its skirt across pebbles. You screech,
You pluck at feathers. Gentlewoman,
I possess no pill for you,
No spoon to lick.

Your illness is in dark thoughts.
The night sky bulks up on clouds,
Behind which the evilest stars shine.

Macbeth (5.1.60)

We see which way the stream of time doth run,
And follow it until we're hooked—
Some die old, some die young,
Some in midstream.

We're allotted our seasons
Until, like fish, we're thrown
Onto the grassy bank
And clubbed into darkness.

2 Henry IV (4.1.70)

Marry, this is the short and the long of it.
I shall be hanged tomorrow,
At dawn they say, before a court of thirteen crows.
When the rope is pulled and my toes wiggle,
The crows will take to the sky
And circle over me like a halo.

I shall be no saint with a long beard—
Nay, more a puppet with arms
And legs flailing about.

I shall be a curio to the crows,
With my left eye half-shuttered,
My right eye a dead stare.

What shall I look upon?
The inside of a crow's smothering wing,
The blackness of eternity.

The Merry Wives of Windsor (2.2.56)

Doth it not show vilely in me to desire small beer?
I have no ambition but a gentle home,
And within these walls my wife and darling girl.
I drink my share, I eat my buttered bread.
Cheese does stick to me.
The potato softens my belly,
And peppered meat makes me devilishly merry.

I'm a laborer and labor I must.
I hammer the fiery irons for the cooper.
My hands are thick, my beard red as fire.
I begin work in the dark and head home in the dark,
Soot falling from me like a shadow.

On Sundays I visit the graves of my two sons—
Consumptives, they drowned in their beds.
I have tears for them, and for their good-byes.
They have traveled farther than I wish to go.

2 Henry IV (2.2.5–6)

Every one can master a grief but he that has it,
The grief of a husband before his wife's grave
The hardest.

At their sweet will,
Clouds pass, thus striping the trees.
Only then we mortals shall see ourselves skeletal,
Wickedly bent, a snap of brittle limbs.

Yet among the branches a certain hope—
The bundle of nests presently empty
Will come alive in spring with meadowlarks.

Below the trees,
Daffodils push radiantly
From the ugliest mud.

Much Ado About Nothing (3.2.26−7)

And one man in his time plays many parts,
That of a babe on a breast, boy on a hobby horse,
That of young rake, husband if it comes to that,
Father perhaps, jailor if it's his calling,
Hunter, fisherman, falconer . . .

So many hats to wear, each square as a church,
Each with a feather, each with a brim
Against sun, wind and rain.

His shoeprints press into mud
As he trudges from home to his labors,
Shallow evidence that he carved out a living.

As You Like It (2.7.141)

I wasted time, and now doth time waste me.
My legs are weak as withering vines.
My teeth fall like coins.
My eyes leak, my heart does not measure up,
My toe sparks from gout.
I'm old, unlearned. The letter R
Is the same as letter P,
Just with a crutch. I wasted myself
In one pub named The Eel & The River.
I could have been a sailor, or a chimney sweep—
Ay, wind I might have swallowed,
The dirt I might have swallowed!

O dear fate, I lay my head on a table,
Drunk was I. I did love once a good woman
And fathered four children who survived on porridge.

What claim do I have to be buried in earth?
I never worked there, not once.
If a log floats the river Thames,
Think it is I lying prone,
My lips, as in my life in the pub,
Sipping freely all they can.

Richard II (5.5.49)

And many strokes, though with a little axe,
Shall bring down a mighty oak in the course of a day.
The tree cracks, leans, and cries as it falls.

Workers with their scythes
Harvest a field before the rain.
The stalks of wheat lay bundled, sighing from heat.

The gopher is a toothy sojourner.
Yet, he gladly shovels his face into the earth
And tunnels to the roots of his delight,
The carrot patch.

Axe stroke, swinging scythe, groveling face . . .
Hard labor does get its way.

3 Henry VI (2.1.54)

Poor soul, the center of my sinful earth,
I have robbed, I have twice nearly murdered,
I have married and been wicked—
In anger I broke my wife's china and scorched her curtains.
I confessed my sins to the priest,
Though was quiet on the subject of my debaucheries.

I walk in shame, creaking of old leather.
If only my soul could escape this body of mine
And enter the clean wood of a pear tree.
Let this miracle happen in spring
When the blossoms roust open their eyes.
Let the wind carpet the ground
With fluttering beauty, then allow
The bees to sting me,
O my soul, with dutiful kisses.

Sonnet 146 (1)

Sir, I'm a true laborer:
The earth is my collar,
The hoe my staff,
The rooster my clock,
The barn my chapel,
The scythe my harp,
The dog my sentry,
The wagon my ship,
The fields my sea
On which I cast
Hope and seed.

As You Like It (3.2.70)

The wheel is come full circle
And crushes the ant and the ant's armored uncle,
The cricket. It is the same for us.

Though we frolic in youth and in first love,
Through we marry and work earth and iron,
Though we pile up coins,
The wheel will roll and crush us.

We are as every living thing,
Alive one moment, and then, like the ant,
Like the cricket, under death's stony wheel.

King Lear (5.3.176)

Since brevity is the soul of wit,
We may argue that the dead are the wisest
For they let the trees above their graves
Have all the say.

Hamlet (2.2.90)

His worse fault is that he is given to prayer;
The canon should shut his trap
And follow what he prays.
If it's healing, then heal.
If it's love, then love.
If it's forgiveness, shake thy enemy's hand.
If it's riches, then toil!
Let the coins of sweat roll off his back
Into this purse.

But the canon stammers on his knees . . .
O how piously his fingers meet.
O how he scoops the incense
And throws that vapor over his back!
He smells of church pews.
He lives by faith.
He prays himself poor
And works not for a place in heaven.

The Merry Wives of Windsor (1.4.11)

Die single, and thine image dies with thee.
This I heed. Both children—Elizabeth and Margaret,
Two girls sweet as music—died of plague.
My dear husband was swept away in a river.

I'm widowed, alone, thin in my thin clothes.
I count nine cows as my herd.
The chickens look up to me.
Candles I can make, butter and jams.
Mushrooms appear overnight—
But these, I distrust.

Who carries my image forward?
The river flows, the larks return in spring,
The cat creeps home with the same numbered stripes.
Who recalls a woman with a face like a potato
And the poverty-tapered legs of an unlit candle?

Sonnet 3 (14)

There's place and means for every man alive.
Yokel, spoon to your porridge!
Cobbler, scissors to your leather!
Farmer, spark your scythe!

What is our destiny but tears that we equally share?
Mother, snap the sheet in anger
And hang it in the westward wind.
Son, make the flute tweet.
We desire music
In this time of plague.
Daughter, set a pail under the cow—
If the milk is pinkish, kick the pail
And cover the spillage with straw.

Prithee, know your place, or invent your place.
The selfsame sun knows its route
And the stars, pinpricks in the night sky,
Lighten our houses.
Sleep rinses trouble from our tired eyes.

All's Well That Ends Well (4.3.329)

Saint Peter . . . shows me where the bachelors sit.
In heaven, I'll have my teapot and pipe,
And a guitar to rest on my knee—
Three melodic chords I know.

They say that I was not fetching in my youth,
That I was a dolt thick as wood,
Hunchbacked from shrugging my shoulders.
Smartly, one rainy spring, I ran when a goose
Of a woman chased me.

My friends, though, married in all seasons
And brought children into the world—
More trumpeting misery than was necessary.
In old age, my friends, befuddled, kept small garden plots.

I gladly remained a bachelor all my simple life.
I was free as air, free to smoke my pipe.
My knife circled the circumference of an apple
And the peel was unheralded scroll.
I frequented pubs, and I strolled alone—
I farted openly and shook my trousers,
My breezy steps taking away its mellowness.
And for women to love? I had my right hand.

Now I wake to wings attached to my shoulders.
In heaven, I find the daily music is the same.
Here, I discover that muscular gents
And pretty lasses have become unhandsome.
Their bowels, like my shoes, leak
When they stroll around the apple tree.

Three imperfect chords on the guitar . . .
They're all I need to hush the domestic clashes
Of the world below.

Much Ado About Nothing (2.1.44–5)

Thus conscience does make cowards of us all.
Thus the villager does not kill,
Nor bed another man's wife,
Nor steal more apples than he can eat,
Nor drown the newborn in a bucket,
Nor filch a candle from the altar,
Nor dine on meat on Friday,
Nor borrow what he can't repay,
Nor speak insensibly of the Lord,
Nor hack off minutes from an hour of work,
Nor whistle a pig home
And run a knife into its belly.

The villager hesitates.
He appraises the bee entering a flower.
He spies squirrels hording acorns—
This seems just, for the smallest creatures should eat.

The villager could never lie, thieve, or murder.
His Christ is above, even at the edge of clouds!
But how could he possibly sleep
With thoughts clean as clearest water
In these happiest of times—
His children, he sees, have come running.

Hamlet (3.1.83)

We are such stuff . . . rounded with a sleep,
But before this eternal sleep,
Our loved ones look away.
To witness death is painful.
The last sigh, the gargle of words,
The nostrils an engine of snorts,
The eyes springing open,
The eyes that close and squeeze
A painful tear.

The last snort of life may move
Nothing grander than a wayward feather,
The weight of thy detachable spirit.

The Tempest (4.1.156–8)

ABOUT THE AUTHOR

Gary Soto, poet and essayist, is the author of dozens of books, including *The Elements of San Joaquin, Junior College, What Poets Are Like, A Summer Life, Living Up the Street,* and *New and Selected Poems,* a finalist for the National Book Award. His poem "Oranges" is the most anthologized poem in contemporary literature. He has received fellowships from the National Endowment for the Arts and the Guggenheim Foundation. In 1995, he was NBC's "Person of the Week." The Gary Soto Literary Museum is located at Fresno City College, where in 1972 he began to write poetry. After a romantic rejection in his sophomore year, he turned to Shakespeare to repair his heart. Years later and fully recovered, he lives with his wife, Carolyn, in Berkeley, California.